GETTING TO KNOW THE WORLD'S GREATEST ARTISTS

# N O R M A N
# ROCKWELL

WRITTEN AND ILLUSTRATED BY MIKE VENEZIA

**CHILDREN'S PRESS®**
A DIVISION OF GROLIER PUBLISHING
NEW YORK   LONDON   HONG KONG   SYDNEY
DANBURY, CONNECTICUT

To the memory of my grandfather, Jack Strothers

Colorist for illustrations: Liz Venezia

Library of Congress Cataloging-in-Publication Data

Venezia, Mike.
  Norman Rockwell  /  written and illustrated by Mike Venezia.
    p.  cm. — (Getting to know the world's greatest artists)
  Summary:  Examines the life and work of the twentieth-century artist
Norman Rockwell, who painted familiar everyday scenes that people felt were part
of their own lives.
  ISBN 0-516-21594-9 (lib. bdg.)  0-516-27158-X (pbk.)
  1. Rockwell, Norman, 1894-1978—Juvenile literature. 2. Painters—United
States—Biography—Juvenile literature. [1. Rockwell, Norman, 1894-1978. 2. Artists.
3. Painting, American. 4. Art appreciation.] I. Title.
ND237.R68 V46 2000
759.13-dc21
  [B]                                                                    99-058036
                                                                              CIP
                                                                               AC

Visit Children's Press on the Internet at:
http://publishing.grolier.com

Norman Rockwell was born in New York City in 1894. For more than sixty years, he painted familiar, everyday scenes that people felt were part of their own lives. By the time he died in 1978, Norman Rockwell had become one of America's all-time favorite artists.

Time to Retire: Old Man with Shopping Basket, by Norman Rockwell. 1925. Oil on canvas. 32 x 26.5 in. Signed lower right: Norman Rockwell. Fisk Tire Company: automobile tire advertisement. Private Collection. Reproduced: *Saturday Evening Post*, 7 February, 1925, p. 141. © Norman Rockwell Museum at Stockbridge.

Something to Be Thankful For (Pilgrim with Gun), by Norman Rockwell. 1922. Signed lower right: Norman Rockwell. Interwoven Stockings: sock advertisement. Whereabouts unknown. Reproduced: *Saturday Evening Post*, 18 November, 1922, p. 76. © Norman Rockwell Museum at Stockbridge.

Norman Rockwell's most famous pictures are illustrations he made for books, advertisements, and, especially, magazine covers.

The Saturday Evening

# POST

September 20, 1958 - 15¢

## Mickey Cohen:
## The Private Life of a Hood
By Dean Jennings

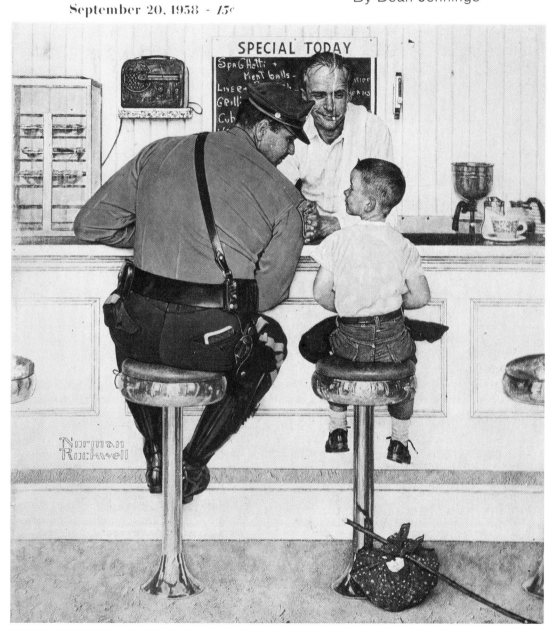

*The Runaway*, by Norman Rockwell. 1958. *Saturday Evening Post*, September 20, 1958.
© Curtis Publishing, Indianapolis, IN.

THE SATURDAY EVENING **POST**

OVERSEAS EDITION FOR NOVEMBER, 1945

OVERSEAS EDITION FOR THE ARMED FORCES DISTRIBUTED TO THE U. S. ARMY BY THE SPECIAL SERVICES DIVISION, A. S. F., TO THE U. S. MARINE CORPS BY "THE LEATHERNECK" AND TO THE NAVY BY THE BUREAU OF NAVAL PERSONNEL, U. S. NAVY

NOT FOR SALE

*Homecoming,* by Norman Rockwell. 1945. *Saturday Evening Post,* October 13, 1945. © Curtis Publishing, Indianapolis, IN.

Illustrations are pictures that help tell a story. Usually, book publishers or advertising agencies ask artists to do illustrations, and then pay them for their work.

During Norman Rockwell's time, important
art critics didn't take illustrators seriously
or consider their works to be fine art. This
snobby attitude always disappointed Norman.
He felt that great illustrations were every
bit as important as great museum paintings.

Some of the first drawings Norman
remembered making were scenes from books
by Charles Dickens. On cold winter nights
when Norman was four or five years old,
his father would read to the family around
the dining-room table.

In the warm glow of a gas lamp, Norman
would try his best to draw characters
described in books like *David Copperfield*
and *Oliver Twist*.

Norman Rockwell (right), 1905. Photographer unknown. © Norman Rockwell Museum at Stockbridge.

Norman grew up in a pretty rough and tough neighborhood. He was lucky to be able to draw. It was about the only thing he was good at. Norman was always super-skinny and terrible at sports.

To make matters worse, his older brother Jarvis was the best athlete in the neighborhood. Without art, Norman felt kids would have just thought of him as a "skinny, pigeon-toed, narrow-shouldered lump."

## Two Knights do battle before Cameliard

Norman knew he wanted to be an artist for as long as he could remember. When he was sixteen, he decided to leave high school and study art seriously. Norman went to several art schools in New York City, including the Art Students' League. This school was started by one of Norman's favorite art heroes, Howard Pyle.

*The Coming of Lancaster,* by Howard Pyle. 1908. Oil on canvas. 35 1/2 x 23 1/4 in. *Harper's Monthly Magazine,* Howard Pyle Collection. © Delaware Museum of Art.

*The Flying Dutchman,* by Howard Pyle. Oil on canvas. Museum Purchase, 1912. *Collier's Weekly,* Dec. 8, 1900. © Delaware Museum of Art.

Norman thought Howard Pyle was one of the greatest illustrators ever. He loved the detail Pyle used in his works. Howard Pyle's drawings seem so real, they give you the feeling that Pyle might have been right there drawing during an adventure with pirates or King Arthur and his knights.

*The Smoke Signal,* by Frederic Remington. 1908. Oil on canvas. 30 3/8 x 48 1/4 in.
© Amon Carter Museum, Fort Worth, Texas.

Norman admired other illustrators too.
He was influenced by Frederic Remington,
Charles Dana Gibson, and J. C. Leyendecker.

*Couple on Deck*, by Charles Dana Gibson. 1897. Ink on paper. 18 1/4 x 27 in. © 2000, by ASaP of Holderness, NH 03245. © American Illustrators Gallery, New York City.

*Thanksgiving - Pilgrim and Football Player*, by J. C. Leyendecker. 1928. Oil on canvas. 28 x 22 in. © 2000, by ASaP of Holderness, NH 03245. *Saturday Evening Post*, November 24, 1928. © American Illustrators Gallery, New York City.

These artists worked during a time in art history known as the Golden Age of Illustration. They had a way of bringing the characters in a story to life and making you feel part of the adventure. Norman Rockwell dreamed of being able to do the same thing someday.

*Self-Portrait*, by Rembrandt. 1660. Oil on canvas.
31 5/8 x 26 1/2 in. Bequest of Benjamin Altman, 1913.
© Metropolitan Museum of Art.

*The Harvesters*, by Pieter Bruegel the Elder. Oil on wood.
46 1/2 x 63 1/4 in. Rogers Fund, 1919. © Metropolitan
Museum of Art.

Norman also enjoyed the work of great master artists from the past. New York City had plenty of art museums where Norman could go to see paintings by Rembrandt, Jan Vermeer, and Pieter Bruegel. It's easy to see the effect these great artists had on some of Norman's paintings.

*Young Woman with a Water Jug,* by Jan Vermeer.
Oil on canvas. 18 x 16 in. Marquand Collection,
Gift of Henry G. Marquand, 1889.
© Metropolitan Museum of Art.

*Painting the Little House*, by Norman Rockwell. 1921. Oil on canvas. 28 x 24 in. Signed lower left: Norman Rockwell.
Save the Surface Campaign: best title contest. Collection of Harry Bassett Holt; Mr. & Mrs. William F. Cooke, Jr.;
Ernest Trig family. Reproduced: *Saturday Evening Post*, 31 December, 1921, p. 67. See Plate 45. © Norman Rockwell
Museum at Stockbridge.

Norman Rockwell was also influenced by his memories of family summer trips. Each year, the Rockwells spent a few weeks in the country. Norman loved playing in the fresh, clean air and wide-open spaces. He especially enjoyed the friendly people he met.

Norman was much happier there than in the overcrowded, dirty, and unfriendly city. Early on, Norman Rockwell decided his artwork would show life only as he would like it to be.

Teachers at the Art Students' League liked Norman. They saw he had talent and was one of the hardest workers there. One teacher helped Norman get his first big art job. It was doing illustrations for a children's book called *Tell-Me-Why Stories*. With the money he made, Norman rented a studio.

*The Camp Book "It is not all of Scouting to scout,"*
by Norman Rockwell. 1913. Signed lower right
center: Norman P. Rockwell 1913. Edward Cave,
*The Boyscout Camp Book*, New York: Doubleday,
Page & Company, 1914, frontis piece. Reproduced:
Buechner, illus. 74 © Norman Rockwell Museum
at Stockbridge.

*The Hike Book, "I'd give my other leg to belong to your
troop!"*, by Norman Rockwell. 1913. Signed lower
right: Norman P. Rockwell. Hike Book, p. 36.
© Norman Rockwell Museum at Stockbridge.

He got more jobs right away. The editor
of *Boy's Life* magazine asked him to do
some drawings for a camping handbook.
The editor liked the illustrations so much
that he offered Norman a job as art director
of *Boy's Life*. At the age of nineteen, Norman
Rockwell had the important job of making
illustrations and deciding how the entire
magazine should look.

Norman Rockwell's dream of becoming a top illustrator was coming true. He was a hard worker and was busy all the time, drawing and painting pictures for ads, books, and magazines. Norman had one dream, though, that was so big, he was almost afraid to try for it. That dream was to illustrate a front cover for the *Saturday Evening Post*.

The *Post* was the most popular magazine in the United States. It was started in 1728 by Benjamin Franklin. Only the best artists were asked to illustrate *Post* covers. The *Post* cover on the next page was done by J. C. Leyendecker, one of Norman's favorite artists.

*Baby New Year*, by J. C. Leyendecker. 1936. *Saturday Evening Post*, January 2, 1937.
© Curtis Publishing, Indianapolis, IN.

Fortunately, Norman shared a studio at this time with an artist friend who encouraged him to show his work to the *Post* magazine people. After months of putting it off, Norman gathered up his courage and a few illustration samples and went to the magazine office.

He thought he'd never sell his work, and was so nervous he was soaked with sweat. But on that day, Norman Rockwell got the surprise of his life. The editor at the *Post* loved Norman's work!

*Boy Pushing Baby Carriage, (aka Salutation),* by Norman Rockwell. 1916. *Saturday Evening Post,* May 20, 1916. © Curtis Publishing, Indianapolis, IN.

Norman's first *Post* cover showed two boys making fun of a third boy who has been forced to babysit and can't play. Norman ended up doing more than three hundred covers for the *Saturday Evening Post.*

*Boy on High Dive*, by Norman Rockwell. 1947. Oil on canvas. 35 x 27 in. © 2000, by ASaP of Holderness, NH, 03245. © American Illustrators Gallery, New York City.

Most of Norman's illustrations show his sense of humor and love of people.

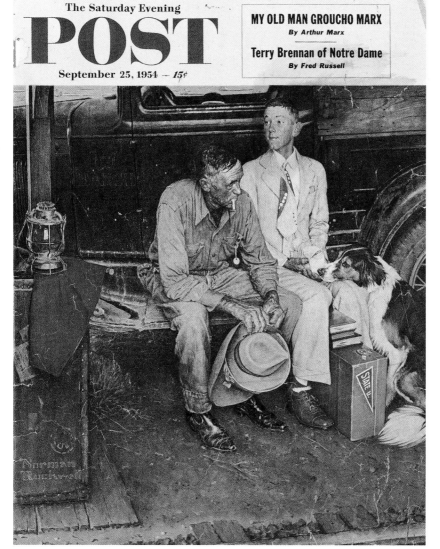

*Breaking Home Ties (Boy and Father Sitting on Truck),* by Norman Rockwell. 1954. Oil on canvas. Signed lower left: Norman Rockwell. *Saturday Evening Post:* 25 September, 1954, cover. Private Collection. Reproduced: Album, p. 143; America illus, 1963; Buechner, illus. 487; Retrospective, p. 113 Photo courtesy of Harry N. Abrams Inc. © Norman Rockwell Museum at Stockbridge.

One thing that makes Norman Rockwell's illustrations so wonderful is the way they tell a story without words.

Norman had a way of designing his pictures so that everything he shows draws your attention to the main idea.

*The Homecoming,* by Norman Rockwell. 1945. Oil on canvas. 28 x 22 in. Signed lower right: Norman Rockwell. *Saturday Evening Post:* 26 May 1945, cover. Collection of Mrs. Edith K. Hibbs. Reproduced: Album, p. 2; America, illus. 244; Buechner, illus. 410, 417; Retrospective, p. 84. © Norman Rockwell Museum at Stockbridge.

*Going & Coming,* by Norman Rockwell. 1947. Oil on canvas. Upper canvas 16 X 31.5 in. Lower canvas 16 x 31.5 in. Signed lower right center: Norman Rockwell, 1947. *Saturday Evening Post:* 30 August, 1947, cover. Norman Rockwell Paintings Trust at Old Corner House. Reproduced: Album, p. 48; America illus. 129. © Norman Rockwell Museum at Stockbridge.

*Saying Grace,* by Norman Rockwell. 1951. Oil on canvas. 42 x 40 in. Curtis Publishing Co. © Norman Rockwell Museum at Stockbridge.

Norman was very careful to make sure all the details that went into his illustrations were as authentic as possible, from a little girl's bubble gum to the well-worn curtains and floor tiles in a restaurant.

Norman filled his paintings with tons of familiar and interesting objects. It's fun to keep looking at his pictures over and over again to see if you missed anything.

Norman Rockwell could draw people and objects as well as any great artist. He used his special talent, along with an original sense of humor, to show that people all over the world were really pretty good.

**Works of art in this book can be seen at the following places:**

Amon Carter Museum, Fort Worth, Texas

Delaware Museum of Art, Wilmington, Delaware

Metropolitan Museum of Art, New York, New York

Norman Rockwell Museum at Stockbridge, Stockbridge, Massachusetts